Meadowbrook Middle School
12320 Meadowbrook Lane
Poway, CA 92064

Uncharted, Unexplored, and Unexplained

Scientific Advancements of the 19th Century

Henry Cavendish

and the Discovery of Hydrogen

Mitchell Lane
PUBLISHERS

P.O. Box 196
Hockessin, Delaware 19707

Uncharted, Unexplored, and Unexplained

Scientific Advancements of the 19th Century

Visit us on the web: www.mitchelllane.com
Comments? email us: mitchelllane@mitchelllane.com

Henry Cavendish
and the Discovery of Hydrogen

Josepha Sherman

Scientific Advancements of the 19th Century

Copyright © 2005 by Mitchell Lane Publishers, Inc. All rights reserved. No part of this book may be reproduced without written permission from the publisher. Printed and bound in the United States of America.

Printing   1   2   3   4   5   6   7   8
        Library of Congress Cataloging-in-Publication Data
Sherman, Josepha.
    Henry Cavendish and the Discovery of Hydrogen
        p. cm. — (Uncharted, unexplored, and unexplained)
    Includes bibliographical references and index.
    ISBN 1-58415-368-7 (lib. bound)
    1. Cavendish, Henry, 1731–1810—Juvenile literature. 2. Chemists—Great Britain—Biography—Juvenile literature. 3. Hydrogen—Juvenile literature. I. Title. II. Series.
QD22.C4S48 2005
540'.92—dc22
[B]
                                                                    2004024614

ABOUT THE AUTHOR: Josepha Sherman is a professional fantasy and science fiction writer, a Star Trek novelist, a children's writer, and a nonfiction writer with over 60 books in print and over 150 short stories. She is also a professional folklorist and editor. In addition, she is a native New Yorker, has a degree in archaeology, loves to tinker with computers, follows the New York Mets, and is a horse whisperer who has had a new foal fall asleep on her foot!

PHOTO CREDITS: Cover, pp. 1, 3, 6, 25, 28—SCETI Collection/Edgar Fahs Smith Collection; p. 9—Omikron/Photo Researchers; pp. 10, 31, 38, 41—Jamie Kondrchek; p. 12—Graeme Robertson/Getty Images; pp. 17, 20, 33, 34—Library of Congress; p. 35—Miskolci; p. 36—Newtonian Mechanics.

PUBLISHER'S NOTE: This story is based on the author's extensive research, which she believes to be accurate. Documentation of such research is contained on page 47.

The internet sites referenced herein were active as of the publication date. Due to the fleeting nature of some web sites, we cannot guarantee they will all be active when you are reading this book.

Uncharted, Unexplored, and Unexplained

Scientific Advancements of the 19th Century

Henry Cavendish

and the Discovery of Hydrogen

*For Your Information

This is the only known authentic portrait of Henry Cavendish. It was probably sketched without his knowledge. He is seen wearing his familiar old-fashioned outfit with its tricorn hat.

1

The Shy Scientist

The year was 1766. As they did once a week, a group of scientists gathered in the meeting hall of the Royal Society, an association of English scientists. The meeting hall was a room in Gresham College in London, where some of them taught. The men came from all branches of science—astronomy, mathematics, chemistry, physics, and more. They all looked forward to the chance to talk over their research, show each other the experiments they had conducted, and read papers to the group about their latest findings.

Suddenly, a strange, thin figure hurried through their midst. Even though he was only in his mid-30s, he wore an old-fashioned suit of faded gray-green fabric and a cocked three-cornered hat that had been out of style for many years. He never looked directly at any of them. He wouldn't meet anyone's gaze, either. But the weird, slightly rumpled-looking man acted as if he knew where he was and why he was there.

"Who is that strange fellow?" one scientist asked another in confusion.

"Why, that man is none other than Mr. Henry Cavendish," the other replied.

"'Mister?' Surely you mean *Lord* Henry Cavendish! Is he not a member of that noble family?"

"He is, indeed, sir, but Mr. Cavendish refuses to use the title. He is only interested in matters of science."

"How very odd!"

Mr. Henry Cavendish was very odd, indeed. He lived and worked alone, although he did share the great Cavendish house in London with his father and their servants. He allowed absolutely no one to visit him. The man avoided seeing even the servants. If he needed them to do something for him, he would leave notes. He hardly ever went out, except to these weekly meetings of the Royal Society, of which he was a member. When he did visit the Royal Society, though, Mr. Cavendish hardly ever spoke to anyone. If he was suddenly faced with someone he did not know, he would scurry away with a shrill small cry of alarm.

"It is said of him," the scientists murmured to each other, "that Mr. Cavendish does not love or hate anyone."

"Indeed. He does not seem able to form strong emotions of any sort. He does not know hope or fear."

"He never even attends any church."

"Mr. Cavendish does seem to fear most human contact."

Even with all their puzzled discussions about him, his fellow scientists still did respect this oddest member of the Royal Society. They knew that for all his strange shyness, odd habits, and old-fashioned clothing, Mr. Henry Cavendish was still a brilliant man. He was amazingly knowledgeable in physics, chemistry, and just about any other scientific subject that took his interest.

Today the word had gone out to all the members of the Royal Society that Mr. Cavendish was about to deliver his first published paper. It was a most important paper. In fact, it was one that might prove him a genius. Henry Cavendish had discovered that air was not a complete element in itself. It could be divided into smaller parts. It was a discovery that would, in time, change the way that scientists looked upon the world.[1]

Henry Cavendish's laboratory at the University of Cambridge. It looks horribly cluttered and old-fashioned by modern standards. But it was just the way he wanted it.

The Royal Society is a famous organization of British scientists. This is a photo of the Royal Society headquarters as they look today. The building used in Henry Cavendish's day was much smaller.

The Royal Society

The Royal Society originated in the 1640s, when a group of scientists started meeting informally in London to discuss their various scholarly interests and compare their findings. The scientists enjoyed their meetings so much that they started getting together once a week. On November 28, 1660, they decided to turn their group into a society for "the Promoting of Physico-Mathematical Experimental Learning."

In 1661, the group came up with a name for their organization. It would be the Royal Society of London, although it soon became known just as the Royal Society. Voting members would be elected, and would be called Fellows of the Royal Society.

The members of the new society needed a regular place to hold their meetings. It didn't seem right to hold them in someone's home, especially since the group consisted of more than thirty members. That was too many people to fit comfortably into one room. A meeting hall in Gresham College in London became their official location.

In 1662 the British government gave the Royal Society a license to publish books. Three years later, the Society began publishing a scholarly magazine, Philosophical Transactions. The magazine is still in existence, making it the oldest continually published scientific journal in the world.

In 1666, the Great Fire of London burned down much of the city. The Royal Society survived the fire, but was forced to move to a temporary home, Arundel House. It was the home of the Duke of Norfolk, a member of the Society. By 1710, funding came in for them to move into two houses in Crane Court.

The Royal Society now makes its headquarters at 6 Carlton House Terrace, London. It is a professional academy of scientists with a staff of over 120 men and women. Its main missions in the twenty-first century are to promote public understanding of the sciences and to promote scientific research. The Royal Society offers grants and funds to promising research, presents lectures, and awards prizes to scientists around the world.

11

Cambridge University is one of the top universities in the world. It was famous in Henry Cavendish's day, too. It is made up of several colleges in which students study everything from the arts to science.

2

Born to the Nobility

Lord Charles Cavendish, second son of the Duke of Devonshire, must have been a very happy man on October 10, 1731. His family was important in society and related to many of the highest ranking members of the English nobility. He had a fine reputation as a mathematician in the Royal Society, and his studies of physics and chemistry were also going well. His portrait shows a keen-eyed, intelligent face. But most important this day was the joyous news that his wife, Lady Anne Cavendish, had just given birth to their first child, a son. The baby was christened Henry, a common name in the Cavendish family.

But things weren't quite as happy with the Cavendish family as they may have seemed. Lady Anne's portrait shows a thin, fragile-looking young woman with only the hint of a smile on her face. Because Lady Anne was in poor health, the family had moved from the Cavendish family estate near London to the small city of Nice (pronounced NEESE) soon after the marriage took place. Nice is part of what is now called the Riviera, in southern France. The region's mild weather and the clean salt air from the nearby Mediterranean Sea were thought to be better for her health. Sadly, though, the change of climate wasn't enough to really help her. Lady Anne died in 1733, not long after giving birth to Henry's brother, Frederick. She was only 27.

There are no records of whether or not Lord Charles Cavendish had ever loved his wife, or whether he truly mourned her loss. He is said to have been a cool, remote, almost withdrawn person. All that is known is that he took his two sons back to England as soon as Frederick was old enough to travel safely, and that he never married again. There were rumors among his neighbors that he actually preferred to be alone. That way he could concentrate on his scientific studies without interruptions.

There also aren't any records of what Henry was like as a boy. In the eighteenth century, child care for the nobility usually meant that the children were kept away from adults and cared for by the family servants. Henry and his younger brother probably fit into this pattern, particularly since Lord Cavendish no longer had a wife to watch over them. Perhaps Henry wasn't treated very well by the servants. An unhappy childhood would help to explain how strange and silent he was as an adult.

In 1742, when he was eleven years old, Henry was sent to Hackney Academy, a boarding school located just outside of London. It was an exclusive private school that was ruled over by a stern but knowledgeable scholar named Peter Newcome. Many boys from aristocratic families were sent to the academy to get a good education. Only boys went to the school. In those days, girls were expected to learn at home.

Henry probably already had developed an interest in his father's studies in the sciences, but his time at Hackney Academy would have given the boy the grounding in logical thinking that a scientist needs. Because there are no records of his school years, we can only guess at what he actually learned and how he felt about school and his schoolmates. He was probably very bright at his studies, but very shy about making friends—if, indeed, he made any.

The next appearance of Henry Cavendish in the records of any school occurs in 1749. That was the year when he began attending St. Peter's College, which is part of Cambridge University in Cambridge, England. Cambridge University is one of the oldest colleges in the world, dating back to the early years of the thirteenth century, and it is the largest university in England. By the time that Henry was admitted to Cambridge, the subjects available for him to study would probably have included mathematics, chemistry, astronomy, geometry, philosophy, and the arts.

Henry studied at the university for more than three years—but again, there are no records of those years. We don't know what he actually did study, how he did on exams, or how he got along with the other students. It's easy to picture him sitting alone in his room, studying, ignoring everyone around him, and never attending any social gatherings. All that is known for sure is that Henry left Cambridge without gaining a degree. No one knows why. However, it wasn't unusual for the sons of aristocratic families to leave school without obtaining a degree. After all, they weren't expected to ever have to work for a living.

After leaving college, young men from noble families in England normally traveled about continental Europe. In fact, such a post-college experience actually came to have a special name. It was known as the "Grand Tour." Allowing young men who were newly out of the confines of college to experience more than their own culture was supposed to make them wiser about the world and its people—and to give them a chance to grow up a little on their own. Of course, it also let them have a great deal of fun, although they were expected to stay out of any real trouble.

Staying out of trouble probably was easy for Henry. He was already showing signs of a weird and humorless adulthood. He was a strange, silent young man, far more quiet than what is generally considered normal. So too, it appears, was his brother Frederick, who accompanied him. Frederick had followed Henry to Cambridge. Unfortunately, he fell out of a window soon after his arrival there. The accident resulted in a permanent dent in his forehead and perhaps some brain damage. An odd incident at the beginning of their tour illustrates their relationship. The two brothers had just landed in France. They happened to pass a funeral with an open coffin.

Frederick is supposed to have said to Henry, "Did you see the corpse?"

Henry is said to have answered, "Yes, I did."

That may have been the only thing the brothers said to each other for the rest of the trip, which seems to have been considerably shorter than traditional Grand Tours. Unlike their father, whose own Grand Tour lasted three and a half years, the brothers were gone for a relatively short time. Apparently they only went as far as Paris. According to some sources, they never spoke to each other again in all their lives after they returned to England.[1] Others describe their relationship as "cordial but distant."[2]

Henry went to live with his father in the family home on Great Marlborough Street in London. The house was a large, rambling place. It really was far too big for just two adults, but it was a mansion in which Henry could be as silent and solitary as he wished.

By now, though, Henry clearly shared his father's passion for scientific research. For the next ten years, father and son worked together in apparent perfect contentment on studies of the stars and planets, extensive and detailed observations about the weather, and experiments that dealt with the nature of water and the expansion of steam with heat. Today, we take such things as steam heat and steam engines for granted, or even look at them as being old-fashioned. In Henry's day, the idea of using steam power was still very new and fascinating. In fact, even though an early type of steam engine had been invented in 1698 by Thomas Savery, an English military engineer, the nature of steam itself—how and why it was created and what it actually was—wasn't yet fully understood.

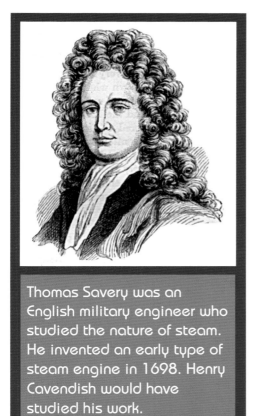

Thomas Savery was an English military engineer who studied the nature of steam. He invented an early type of steam engine in 1698. Henry Cavendish would have studied his work.

Lord Charles was also interested in another mysterious subject: electricity. It may not seem mysterious in the twenty-first century, but that era was almost a hundred years before the invention of electric lights. No one knew much about electricity, or what could be done with it. Henry helped his father with his research, then started working on his own experiments with electricity.

At that time, the study of electricity was still so new that Henry didn't have any instruments for making accurate measurements of electric current. His solution fell into the "Don't try this at home" category. Henry simply shocked himself, and estimated the force of the current from the resulting pain and how far it traveled up his arms: fingers, hands, elbows, and finally to the shoulders. That he might have electrocuted himself in the middle of his experiments doesn't seem to have occurred to him.

Unfortunately, Henry seems to have just been carrying out these experiments to satisfy his own curiosity. He never published the results of most of his experiments on electrical force or how electricity can be conducted. These results anticipated the findings that began to be made several decades later. Henry's experiments probably would have brought him fame, and might even have speeded up the commercial use of electricity. But most of them were published long after his death.

It wasn't surprising that Henry should be so determined to learn about the unknown. His father was only one of many scientists in England in the eighteenth century. The country was changing quickly. Explorers were discovering more about the rest of the world, the New World was being settled by men who—within Henry's lifetime—would establish the United States of America, and merchants were bringing back goods from all over. Everyone wanted to know more about everything there was to learn. New discoveries seemed to be made every day, and relatively recent inventions such as the telescope and microscope were adding to the excitement by allowing scientists to peer into the heavens and observe minute forms of life far too small to be visible to the naked eye. Even non-scientists were fascinated by what was being discovered, even if they didn't always understand the discoveries. Professor John Playfair, a member of the Royal Society, noted in his journal (with a touch of humor) that "Chemistry is the *rage* in London at present."[3]

Sponsored by his father, who had become a member when he was twenty-three, Henry joined the Royal Society in 1760. The organization played an important role in the lives of both men. As biographers Christa Jungnickel and Russell McCormmach observe, "Election to the Royal Society was the most important event in Lord Charles Cavendish's public life. For his son Henry it was decisive, for without his father in the Royal Society, it is hard to imagine the shy Henry entering science in any public way and, perhaps, doing science at all."[4]

For Henry, membership in the Royal Society also had a practical value. Going to the weekly dinners was probably his primary social life. Like his father, he brought only the exact amount of money that was needed to pay for the dinners, never a penny more. Even though the Cavendish father and son were far from being poor, Henry's father kept his adult son on a tight budget. Maybe this was done just to teach Henry the value of money. Maybe his father was a bit of a miser. The tight budget might also have been a sign that Henry was being taught not to rely on the outside world for help.

London

London was a swiftly growing city in the eighteenth century. Before Henry Cavendish's time, most English people lived on farms. But two things changed that fact.

First, the population of England was growing rapidly. That meant that more food needed to be grown. Starting around 1750, the government passed hundreds of Enclosure Acts. These laws were meant to turn grazing land back into cultivated farm land by dividing up pastures and enclosing them with fences. Losing their pastureland put a good many farm workers, those who depended on their cows and sheep for a living, out of a job. They fled to the cities, looking for work.

The second reason for the quick move from country to city was that the cities, with their many types of jobs, offered higher wages than farmers could earn in the country. These higher wages particularly attracted young people who didn't want to be farmers and who wanted to live in a place as exciting as London. By the end of the century, London's population had grown to over a million. It was the largest city in England.

Thames River

It was one of the most exciting, too. During the day, business was carried out all over the city. Ships docked on the Thames River brought in exotic cargo from the New World colonies or the mysterious Orient. There were coffeehouses all over London where people would hang out and chat or even talk business, just as people do today. There were shops to visit and shows to enjoy.

The excitement didn't stop when night fell. There were plenty of parks lit by the newly improved oil-burning street lights where people could hear music or dance to it. The many London theatres were always full of plays or musical events.

Of course, with the much larger crowds of people and more money to be had, trouble came in the shape of street gangs and petty thieves. There was also the occasional riot for better wages. But most people agreed that crime was just another part of life in eighteenth century London.

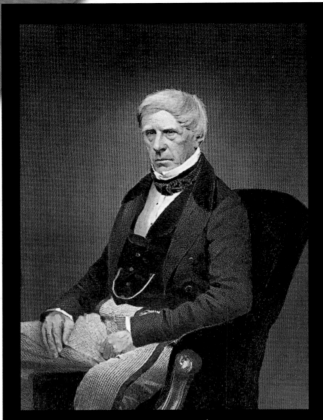

This is a formal portrait of Lord Henry Brougham. It makes him look very grim, indeed. But he was actually a very bright man who tackled many jobs, including lawyer, politician, and writer.

3

The Mysterious Phlogiston

Everyone is going to be shy sometimes. A boy may be nervous about meeting new people or a girl may be scared about facing new things. There's nothing wrong with that. We've all felt at least a little shy on the first day of school or when we're meeting the new kids in camp or at a party. Most people don't let shyness stop them from doing what they really want to do.

Unfortunately, for some people, their shyness becomes too strong a force for them to handle. It gets in the way of what they want to do and stops them from being happy. Shyness can become so powerful, in fact, that it turns into a type of illness.

Henry Cavendish was one of those completely shy people. Being of noble birth only made things worse. He didn't have to work for a living; as a result, he didn't have to be with other people. If he had held a regular job, perhaps Henry would have gotten used to the company of others, and maybe would have even come to like it.

In fact, that terrible, powerful shyness kept Henry from having what we think of as a normal life. He couldn't stand to speak to more than one person at a time, even in the safety of his own house. Henry was so terrified of meeting people by accident that he built himself a private, separate entrance to the house. That way he could come in and go out without ever needing to risk running into anyone else.

Henry's shyness seems to have been at its strongest when it came to women. Part of the problem may have been the fact that he had no mother or sister and that he had gone to an all-male school and university. Henry never actually had a chance to really know any women.

That lack of knowledge only fed his shyness. He was genuinely terrified at the thought of even meeting a woman, let alone being forced to speak to one. Since every house belonging to the nobility of that era had female servants to do the cooking and cleaning, this terror of women posed a real problem for Henry. He solved it by never speaking to any of the women in the house or even letting any of them see him. Instead, Henry gave them their orders for their daily chores in notes and left the notes where they could pick them up. He also left orders in notes for what he wanted for his dinners. Any woman who was unlucky enough to run into him in his house ran the risk of being fired there and then.

Probably very few women would have wanted to run into him. He wasn't the best-looking of men. Henry didn't care very much about how he looked. A small, pale figure, he usually seemed like a person who was of little, if any, importance. He dressed in shabby, often worn-out violet or gray-green suits that were almost a hundred years out of fashion, with high collars and cuffed sleeves. He wore a three-cornered hat that was similarly outdated. He also refused to let anyone call him by his title, as though he felt that it only got in the way. He preferred to be known only by his name: Mr. Cavendish.

He flatly refused to sit for a portrait. As a result, there is only one contemporary image of him, and that was obtained by trickery. An artist named William Alexander arranged to be invited to one of the Royal Society's dinners. He sat next to the pegs where Henry hung his hat and coat, and quickly sketched those items. Then when Henry wasn't looking, Alexander made a quick sketch of him. When he got home that evening, he put all the elements together. Henry never saw the drawing, but his friends did. They all agreed that it was very accurate.

Lord Henry Brougham, who served as a lawyer, a politician, and the Lord Chancellor of England, as well as a writer and biographer, knew Henry personally. He said about Henry that he "probably uttered fewer words in the course of his life than any man."[1]

When he did speak, Henry's voice was thin and shrill, almost a squeak. Professor Playfair, who frequently attended Royal Society meetings and also knew Henry, said that he was "of an awkward appearance . . . he speaks with great difficulty, and hesitation, and very seldom."[2] But the professor, who appreciated Henry's keen intelligence, quickly added that "The gleams of genius break often through this unpromising exterior . . . Mr. Cavendish . . . is the only one [of the Royal Society members] who joins together the knowledge of mathematics, chemistry, and experimental philosophy."[3]

Henry was, indeed, studying many of the scientific puzzles of his century, particularly those in the fields of chemistry and physics. In his time, those two subjects were often combined.

In 1764, he wrote in his personal records about some experiments that he'd conducted with arsenic. It was apparently the first series of chemical experiments that he had undertaken on his own. Henry wasn't at all interested in the nastier side of arsenic, which is its historic use as a poison. He was trying to discover more about its composition and any possible beneficial uses that it might possess.

The following year, Henry performed experiments to learn what heat actually is and how it operates. Everyone already knew that things became hot, of course, but Henry was trying to figure out why heat happened. He also studied how condensation—the water that appears when something cools—is formed.

Just as Henry didn't publish his early findings about the nature of electricity, he didn't publish his findings about these new experiments, either. As a result, no one knew about what he had discovered. That doesn't seem to have bothered him at all. In the case of his heat experiments, they were also being performed by a Scottish chemist, Joseph Black. It may be that Henry's shyness got in his way, making him deliberately delay publication of this work so it wouldn't look as though he was competing with Black. But Henry did seem to be very reluctant to publish anything at all. This reluctance to let anyone see the results of his work may also have been caused by his shyness, or it may have had to do with a fear of being rejected. No one knows the real reason.

However, even Henry couldn't resist publishing some of his major findings in 1766. Entitled "Three Papers, Containing Experiments on Factitious Air," his presentation at the Royal Society was what was so exciting to his fellow members, even as they discussed his odd appearance and habits.

At the end of the seventeenth century, a German scientist named Georg Ernst Stahl (1660–1734) had stated that a mysterious material he called phlogiston was what made materials such as wood and paper burn. The problem was that no one really knew what phlogiston was. No one had been able to study it with any degree of accuracy. Nevertheless, Stahl's phlogiston theory dominated the study of chemistry for much of the eighteenth century. Henry believed in the theory, and the terms he used in his presentation reflected that belief.

The "factitious airs" he referred to in the title were gases that were contained in various metals. He dissolved the metals in acid baths, then collected the gases that escaped and subjected them to a series of careful and very painstaking measurements.

His research centered on two of these gases. One was "fixed air," which today we know as carbon dioxide. He discovered many of its qualities, such as the fact that it could extinguish flames. We still use carbon dioxide in some forms of fire extinguishers.

The second was what he termed "inflammable air." He thought he had discovered true phlogiston. He hadn't. He had discovered hydrogen,

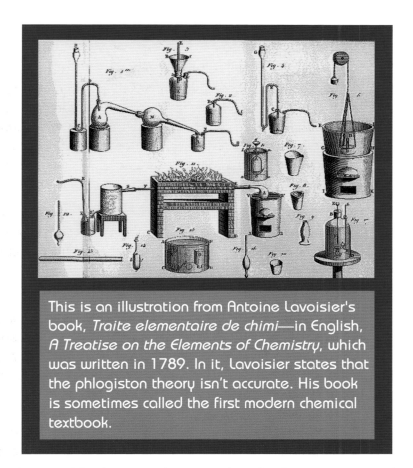

This is an illustration from Antoine Lavoisier's book, *Traite elementaire de chimi*—in English, *A Treatise on the Elements of Chemistry*, which was written in 1789. In it, Lavoisier states that the phlogiston theory isn't accurate. His book is sometimes called the first modern chemical textbook.

although it would take more than two decades for it to receive that name. What was immediately apparent was that Henry had given strong evidence that his "inflammable air" wasn't just a particular variety of air, but an entirely new substance.

The Royal Society was excited about Henry's discoveries. He had just made an enormous breakthrough in the science of chemistry. For his findings, the Society awarded Henry the Copley Medal. The Copley Medal is the Royal Society's highest honor, and it is given for outstanding work in any field of science. It is also the Society's oldest honor, originating in a bequest in 1709 from one of its members and awarded for the first time in 1731.

Awarding the Copley Medal to Henry was certainly justified. As Jungnickel and McCormmach point out, his "experiments on factitious air discredited the old notion of a single, universal air, and in so doing he laid out a new field of discovery. That work alone would entitle Cavendish to a memorable place in the history of science, but he was just beginning."[4]

It took Henry another five years to publish another paper. In 1771, he finally decided to share some of his findings about electricity. He presented them in a paper titled "An Attempt to Explain Some of the Principle Phenomena of Electricity by Means of an Elastic Fluid," in which he stated that "a body can be both positively electrified and undercharged." In other words, a body can contain both a positive and a negative electrical charge.

Five years later, he published his second—and final—paper about his research with electricity. It dealt with the effects produced by the torpedo fish, which used electricity as a weapon. Henry constructed a working model of a torpedo fish, and touched it with pieces of wet shoe leather to simulate the effects of stepping on a real fish while walking along the beach. He must have been proud of his accomplishment. He departed from his usual aversion to company by inviting several noted scientists to visit his laboratory and experience first-hand the same jolts that he had experienced.

He made a further departure from his solitary habits in 1782 when he hired a young scientist named Charles Blagden to serve as his personal assistant. Their professional relationship became personal as well. With Blagden supplying encouragement and making all the necessary arrangements, the two men took a number of trips during the next few years. Even though Blagden left Cavendish's employment seven years later to pursue other interests, they remained lifelong friends.

Asperger's Syndrome

Doctors call the shyness that Henry Cavendish suffered from a pathological shyness. The word "pathological" means "diseased" or "caused by a disease." Pathological shyness is a disease of the mind that makes a person so terrified of other people that he or she completely avoids them.

Hans Asperger

Henry Cavendish may also have been suffering from a brain disorder that is called Asperger's Syndrome. Named after Hans Asperger, the Austrian doctor who first described the disorder in 1944, Asperger's Syndrome is a mild form of autism, or possibly a separate but related illness.

Autism is a brain disorder that usually shows up during the first three years of a person's life. It affects those parts of the brain that control language and the ability to get along with other people. Children and adults with autism usually have difficulty speaking and communicating, and in dealing with other people. They also may show odd repetitive motions, such as continually rocking, or refuse to make any changes in their routines. They often cannot bear eye-to-eye gazes, and often stick to specific, unchanging routines. However, their language skills and ability to think are unaffected.

If Henry did have Asperger's Syndrome, it would explain why he never would look anyone directly in the eye. He wouldn't be able to deal with direct contact. Members of the Royal Society quickly learned that if they wanted to speak with him, they had to look away from his face or stare blankly into space.

Asperger's Syndrome would also explain why Henry insisted that his boots had to be placed in precisely the same spot every night, and why his coat must always be hung on exactly the same peg. It would explain why he followed the same routine every day and ate almost exactly the same meal every night. He may have needed that detailed pattern to help him feel more comfortable.

Asperger's Syndrome could also account for his lack of interest in his personal appearance, but that lack of interest in personal appearance turns up in other people as well. It might simply mean that he just wasn't interested in anything fancy.[5]

27

Antoine Lavoisier was a famous French scientist who lived at the same time as Henry Cavendish. He tested Henry's theories. Here he's portrayed standing in an idealized version of his laboratory.

4

The Wizard of Clapham Common

In 1783, Lord Charles Cavendish, Henry's father, died. In spite of having been kept on such a strict budget by the man for so long, Henry still must have been shocked at losing his father, who had also been his science partner. There are no records, though, to show his emotions—or maybe the lack of emotions.

Henry Cavendish was now completely on his own. He had his father's inheritance. That wasn't all. He also received a very large inheritance from an uncle. Since Henry was younger than many other Cavendishes, further inheritances followed as older relatives died and included Henry in their wills. Henry Cavendish soon found himself extremely wealthy.

But money doesn't seem to have interested him at all, except for the fact that it let him be as solitary as he liked. Henry abandoned the house he and his father had shared. It may have been too big for one man. Perhaps it held painful memories. He moved into a new house—or rather, houses. Henry quickly bought two of them.

The first house he acquired was in London, on Bedford Square, but it didn't wind up as his home. Henry may have found that the house was too close to the city noise and to the never-ending crowds of people.

Instead, he decided that this London house would become his scientific library. He had gathered quite a large collection of books and magazines over the years. With his inheritances, he could now afford to buy any new volumes that he wished. This wasn't a small thing, since most books were expensive by today's standards. Because scientific books and journals were far too expensive in the eighteenth century for many scientists to own, Henry even opened up his private library for other scholars to use—although, being the shy person he was, he didn't stay around to actually meet or talk with them. Henry set the house up as a regular working library, with a librarian, a full book catalogue, and a take-out register. Henry was so careful about keeping this library in proper working order that even when he took one of his books for his own use, he made sure to enter its title into the register.

Henry was not what people would call a very kind-hearted man, or one who freely gave money to charity. But that doesn't seem to have been because he didn't care about those in need. Instead, it may have been because he was so focused on science that he doesn't seem to have realized that there were charities at all unless someone reminded him of them. Once he was reminded, he would almost absent-mindedly donate large sums. When Henry learned that his first librarian, who had retired, was in poor health and needed money, Henry gave the man a considerable amount of money. Representatives of charities who approached him for donations soon learned that he would examine the lists carefully. Then he would write a check equal to the highest amount that he had observed on the list.

The second house that Henry bought was in Clapham Common, a village just outside London. The plain brick building he chose wasn't very unusual or attractive, but it clearly was what he wanted. Though it became his private home, it was far from being a typical residence. A ship's mast rose from the rear, serving as the base for telescopes, thermometers, and other instruments with which he could examine the heavens and continue the studies in meteorology he had begun with his father. A wooden platform on the lawn let Henry climb up into a tree to take other scientific measurements. Henry turned the drawing room, the

This is an old photograph taken of Clapham Common in winter. Today, Clapham Common is cut by a busy main road and is surrounded by homes and businesses. But it still has a park-like feel to it.

eighteenth century version of a living room, into a laboratory. Several of the other rooms became scientific workshops and an astronomical observatory. These arrangements didn't leave very much room for ordinary furniture, but Henry doesn't seem to have cared about anything as unimportant—to him—as a dining room table or chairs.

The people of the village thought that their new neighbor was very strange, and not just because of the changes he'd made to his house. What they found weirdest about him was that they almost never saw him. Henry took a walk every day, but always at dusk, and always alone, walking by choice in the middle of the road—unless he saw someone. In that case, he'd leave the road altogether and hide. When he went out by horse-drawn carriage to the weekly meetings of the Royal Society, he always sat as far back in one corner of the carriage as possible. He didn't want to be seen by anyone. People began whispering to each other that the mysterious Lord Henry Cavendish was a wizard.

Henry's normal day seldom varied. He would start the morning by checking the various thermometers and other instruments around the outside of his house, and write down the data. Then he would retire to his laboratory to continue his scientific studies. In the evening, he would leave the house to take his daily walk. He would end the day by catching up on scientific books and journals. Food didn't particularly interest him. He usually ate mutton for every dinner.

It really upset Henry to have to make any changes to this routine, other than to attend the weekly meeting of the Royal Society. That was an event which he rarely missed. While this quiet, unchanging routine may sound like a boring life, it was exactly what Henry wanted. It gave him plenty of time to think and to conduct his very careful experiments.

Henry put the time for thinking and experimenting to good use. In 1784, he published one of his most famous papers. In it, he described experiments he had conducted with a mixture of his "inflammable air" and a gas that English scientist Joseph Priestley had isolated a decade earlier. This gas, which Priestley called "dephlogisticated air," appeared to be necessary for combustion to take place. Henry demonstrated that when he ignited an electrical spark in a closed jar containing a mixture of the two gases, water was formed.

Famed French scientist Antoine Lavoisier duplicated Henry's experiment and obtained the same results. Lavoisier also renamed the two gases. Because he rejected the phlogiston theory, he gave the name of oxygen to the gas that Priestley had discovered. According to Lavoisier's research, combustion requires oxygen, not phlogiston. Stahl's theory would become history, although its defenders continued to resist Lavoisier's explanation for years.

In Lavoisier's terminology, Henry's "inflammable air" became hydrogen. It is derived from two Greek words: "hydro," meaning water,

Joseph Priestley was another famous scientist of Henry's time. It was Priestley who discovered oxygen—and the way to make carbonated water. That led to the invention of bottled seltzer and sodas.

and "gennan," meaning generating. In other words, hydrogen is "what makes water."

Henry's experiment was a major contribution to scientific knowledge. Up to that point, it had been believed that water was an element, something that could not be divided any further. Henry proved that water was a compound, composed of hydrogen and oxygen. He also established the precise chemical makeup of water. It is composed of two parts of hydrogen and one part of oxygen.

In his further research, Henry found that common air, as well as the air that was brought down by a balloon from the upper atmosphere, consists almost entirely of oxygen and another gas called nitrogen, and established their relative proportions: nearly four parts of nitrogen to one part of oxygen. He also noticed that there was a tiny residue left over when he separated air into oxygen and nitrogen. Although his equipment wasn't powerful enough to identify this residue, his finding was crucial in the discovery of argon and other rare gases more than a century later.

There was another scientific puzzle that was intriguing Henry. While the size of the earth was a well-known fact in his day, no one yet had figured out a way to learn its mass, or weight. About a hundred years earlier, another English scientist, Isaac Newton, had worked out the laws of gravity. He discovered that the force of mutual attraction between two bodies, such as two planets—that is, the pulling force they both have—was related to the distance between them. But Newton had no way of calculating the percentage of this attraction. Without it, he couldn't accurately work out the earth's mass.

Sir Isaac Newton was one of the leading scientists of his day, and is still famous for his discoveries. One of these is the discovery of the laws of gravity. But for all his genius, Newton got into many arguments with other scientists.

Ever since Newton's time, scientists had continued to hunt for a way to measure the Earth's density, or mass. In 1798, Henry used a device called a torsion balance, invented by fellow English scientist John Michell, to find an answer.

The torsion balance is a simple instrument. It is made up of two small lead balls hanging from short wires at each end of a wooden beam. The beam itself is suspended at its midpoint from another wire

This looks like a modern sculpture, or maybe an image of an alien. But it's actually a torsion balance. Although the early ones were made of wood, this one is made of brass and steel.

so that it can twist freely, and its movements can be measured. Two massive lead balls, one near each end of the device, attract the small suspended balls. The movements the small balls make are almost imperceptible. Because the slightest disturbance could interfere with those movements, Henry built a special room to hold all of the equipment. Henry made a hole in the wall, then stood outside and made his observations through a telescope that was aimed through the hole.

His observations were very time-consuming and took nearly a year. When Henry noted the very slight but real movements, he became the first scientist to measure the force of gravitational motions. He was able to make these calculations because he knew the masses of the respective lead balls. That way he could measure the force that balls exerted on one another. Of course, the attractions that he was measuring were tiny, since the whole device was so small. But after all, Isaac Newton had already formulated the law of universal gravitation—gravitation that applied to everything, regardless of size.

Using this formula, Henry was able to calculate the density of the earth. He concluded that the earth weighed 6,600 billion billion tons and had a density of about 5.5 times that of water. The accuracy of his measurements could not be improved upon until more highly advanced equipment was invented in the nineteenth century. The measurements he obtained using relatively primitive equipment remain remarkably close to the modern figures.

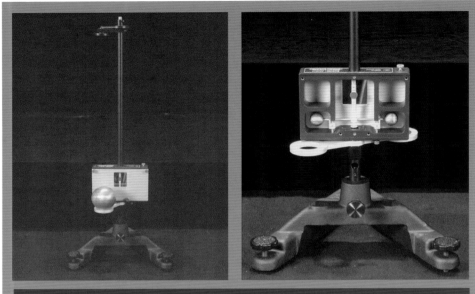

This is the torsion balance that Henry Cavendish used. On the left is a picture of the entire instrument. On the right is a close-up showing the details of construction.

Henry also did some scientific work for the British government. He served on a committee to find the best way to protect a powder magazine—a gunpowder storage site—from lightning. A lightning strike hitting volatile gunpowder would cause a terrible explosion. Henry also studied the strength and durability of different gold alloys in an attempt to help create longer-lasting coins. He even became involved with assuring the accuracy of instruments that measured various weather conditions.

FYInfo

Hydrogen is a tasteless, colorless, odorless gas that burns quickly. It is the most common element in the universe, as scientists believe that hydrogen makes up over 90 percent of all atoms. It makes up nearly 75 percent of the mass of the sun. On earth, there is very little hydrogen in the air we breathe. But hydrogen can be found as part of the chemical combinations that exist in almost all plants and animals—and water.

Hydrogen is an element, which means that it is a basic chemical substance, something that can't be broken down into other chemicals. The hydrogen atom itself is the simplest and smallest of any atom. It is made up of two tiny parts. One, the proton, has a positive charge—it "pulls." The other, the electron, has a negative charge—it "pushes."

When people hear the word "hydrogen," they often think of the hydrogen bomb. This is a terribly powerful weapon. But hydrogen has many peaceful uses as well. It helps in the refining of petroleum into gasoline, and combined with oxygen becomes the fuel for torches that burn hot and bright. Hydrogenated vegetable oils—such as those used in salad dressings and margarine—are healthier than those produced from animal fats. Starting in the late eighteenth century, it was the original fuel for hot air balloons. NASA, the National Aeronautics and Space Agency, uses hydrogen to power space vehicles. It provides more energy than gasoline and its light weight allows these vehicles to carry enough fuel to escape the earth's gravitational pull.

In the future, hydrogen may be used in cleaner fuel for cars and airplanes. Hydrogen can be used to power fuel cells for cars and buses. When hydrogen and oxygen are combined in a fuel cell, they generate electricity and reduce pollution. Some cities, such as New York City, are already experimenting with electric buses.

Since hydrogen is almost always found as part of a compound such as water, scientists believe that there must be easy, inexpensive ways to extract it. They are presently searching for those techniques.[2]

The Institut de France is a world-famous science institution. This photograph shows it as it looks today. But much of it does date from Henry's time.

5

Endings and Beginnings

Henry seems to have performed all of his scientific experiments out of pure curiosity and a burning desire to find out how things worked. He clearly didn't want fame, didn't need any extra money, and he also didn't seem to care whether other people ever knew about his findings or not. The only honor that he ever accepted, other than the awarding of the Copley Medal, was being elected one of the eight foreign associates of the Institut de France in 1803.

Though Henry did sometimes write for publication—though only, it seems, when he wanted to do so—most of his scientific work never was published during his lifetime. In fact, during his entire career as a scientist, Henry published only twenty articles and no books. By contrast, other scientists may publish over a hundred articles and books during their lifetimes.

Throughout all his life, Henry seemed barely to change. He went through his seventies looking and acting almost exactly as he had when he was a younger man, and never seemed to even get sick.

But early in 1810, time finally ran out for Henry Cavendish. On February 24th, he came home to Clapham Common and fell into bed with what was probably his only serious illness. Weakened by it and understanding what was happening to him at last, Henry called his valet, his personal servant, to his bed. Henry is recorded as saying, "Mind what I say, I am going to die. When I am dead, but not until then, go to Lord George Cavendish [the son of a cousin] and tell him of the event. Go!"[1]

Although no one can say for sure what was going on in Henry's mind just then, he apparently wanted to be left alone so that he could investigate for himself, without any outside interruptions, the last of his experiments: what dying was like. Like many of his other experiments, this was one he wished to keep to himself.

When the servant returned, Henry was dead.

Henry Cavendish was buried in Derby Cathedral, in the Cavendish family vault. He left all of his money to his relatives, but oddly enough, left nothing to science. Why this happened, when his entire life centered on science, no one knows. One likely explanation is that Henry may have felt that his wealth had come from his family. It was therefore fitting that he gave it back to his family. In the nineteenth century, the Cavendish family fixed that oversight by providing the necessary funding to establish the Cavendish Laboratory at Cambridge University.

Henry's science library was left to another relative, the Duke of Devonshire. He moved it to Chatsworth House, which is located in central England. One of the greatest private libraries in the world, the Library at Chatsworth currently contains over 30,000 books. The collection of Henry's science books is still there, together with some of the instruments he used.

Was Henry Cavendish really an unhappy man? Charles Blagden, who was perhaps Henry's only real friend, said, "The love of truth was sufficient to fill his mind."[2]

Maybe that was the whole story. Maybe Henry's powerful love for learning really was so great that there wasn't room in his thoughts for anything else. It sounds like a lonely way to live. But maybe he didn't miss what he didn't have.

Maybe in his own odd, solitary, brilliant way, Mr. Henry Cavendish was a happy man after all.

Nowadays, Chatsworth House is open to the public except for four weeks in December and January. It is a true mansion, and has beautiful gardens as well. There are also some spectacular fountains.

Here is a look into the Chatsworth Library as it is today. The Library holds more than 17,000 leather-bound books from the 16th to the 19th centuries. Scholars can make appointments to study in it.

Cavendish Laboratory at
Cambridge University

Named after Henry Cavendish, the Cavendish Laboratory is the Department of Physics of the University of Cambridge in England. It was built in 1873 with money from one of Henry's relatives, William Cavendish. Its purpose was to be a teaching laboratory where graduate students would be able to learn about the sciences, especially physics.

Over the last century, the Cavendish Laboratory has honored its namesake. While physics remains the most important subject, other sciences such as biology, astronomy, and electronics also have facilities there.

One of the most important discoveries in modern science was made in the Cavendish Laboratory. Two research scientists working there, Francis Crick and James Watson, were very interested in figuring out how genetic information within the body was transmitted. They believed that DNA (deoxyribonucleic acid), a chemical substance in every cell, could hold the answer. They worked together to find the structure of DNA. In 1953, their model showed that its structure is a double helix, like a twisted ladder. Crick and Watson received the Nobel Prize in 1962 for their work.

They weren't alone in receiving high honors. A total of twenty-eight Cavendish scientific researchers have been awarded the prestigious Nobel Prize. They include the men who discovered the three primary particles that compose the atom: Joseph John Thomson (electron), Ernest Rutherford (proton), and James Chadwick (neutron).

The Cavendish Laboratory's growth resulted in a move to an expanded site in 1974. There are plans to expand the Cavendish Laboratory even further, as new sciences are added. One of the most recent buildings is the Nanoscience Centre, which opened in 2003 and serves as the home base for studies of the smallest possible technological and biological entities.

The Cavendish Laboratory also fosters an Outreach program to get children interested in science. And it provides programs for adults interested in learning more about science as well.

Chronology

Timeline of Discovery

ca. 100	The Greek philosopher Hero of Alexandria describes his experiments with air and light.
130	The Greek philosopher Ptolemy of Alexandria writes about optics, reflection, and refraction.
1600	English scientist William Gilbert writes *De Magnete*, a book in which he describes the principles of magnetism.
1666	Sir Isaac Newton discovers the essentials of calculus, the law of universal gravitation, and that white light is composed of all the colors of the spectrum.
1733	French scientist Charles François de Cisternay Du Fay discovers two types of static electricity, and that similar electrical charges repel each other while opposite charges attract each other.
1752	American scientist and statesman Benjamin Franklin flies a kite during a storm to prove that lightning is electricity.
1769	James Watt receives a patent for the improvements he makes to the steam engine.
1774	Joseph Priestly discovers "dephlogisticated air," which French scientist Antoine Lavoisier renames oxygen in 1788.
1777	Lavoisier proposes the idea of chemical compounds, which are composed of more than one element.
1800	French scientist Andre-Marie Ampere discovers the properties of a magnetic field that is produced by electric current.
1803	English scientist John Dalton presents the first table of atomic weights.
1807	The first steam-powered vessel, American inventor Robert Fulton's *Clermont*, makes its maiden voyage up the Hudson River.
1813	Swedish scientist Jöns Berzelius develops the symbols for chemical elements that are still in use today.
1869	Russian scientist Dimitri Mendeleyev publishes his periodic table of known elements, which is used to predict the properties of all elements.
1879	American inventor Thomas A. Edison invents the electric light bulb.
1905	German scientist Albert Einstein publishes a paper on the special theory of relativity.
1906	English scientist Joseph J. Thomson receives the Nobel Prize in Physics for his discovery of the electron in 1897.
1911	New Zealand scientist Ernest Rutherford discovers that the positive charge of an atom is concentrated in its nucleus.
1913	Danish scientist Niels Bohr publishes his model of the atom.
1916	Albert Einstein publishes his *General Theory of Relativity*.
1953	James Watson and Francis Crick discover the double helix structure of DNA.
2001	American scientists J. Craig Ventner and Francis Collins jointly publish their decoding of the human genome, the genetic "blueprint" of a human being.
2004	Eight major automakers have entries in California Cruisin' Hydrogen road rally.
2005	Both the Physics at Work exhibition and the Liquid Crystal Elastomer Conference are held at Cavendish Laboratory.

Chapter Notes

Chapter 1   The Shy Scientist
    1. The conversation of the scientists is taken from George Wilson, *The Life and Works of the Honorable Henry Cavendish* (London: The Cavendish Society, 1851).

Chapter 2   Born to Nobility
    1. W.R. Aykroyd, *Three Philosophers: Lavoisier, Priestley and Cavendish* (London: William Heinemann, 1935), p. 72.
    2. Christa Jungnickel and Russell McCormmach, *Cavendish* (Philadelphia: The American Philosophical Society, 1996), p. 77.
    3. John Playfair, *The Works of John Playfair*, edited by J.G. Playfair, 4 volumes, (Edinburgh: Publisher unknown, 1822, chapter one, p. xxxv.)
    4. Jungnickel and McCormmach, p. 56.

Chapter 3   The Mysterious Phlogiston
    1. Henry, Lord Brougham. *Lives of Men of Letters and Science, Who Flourished in the Time of George III* (London: Charles Knight and Co., 1845).
    2. John Playfair, *The Works of John Playfair*, edited by J.G. Playfair, 4 volumes, (Edinburgh: Publisher unknown, 1822), chapter one, p. xxxv.
    3. Ibid.
    4. Christa Jungnickel and Russell McCormmach, *Cavendish* (Philadelphia: The American Philosophical Society, 1996), p. 154.
    5. For more about Asperger's Syndrome and autism, see the Autism Society of America's website, www.autism-society.com.

Chatper 4   The Wizard of Clapham Common
    1. For more about the possible uses of hydrogen, see Peter Hoffman, *Tomorrow's Energy: Hydrogen, Fuel Cells, and the Prospects for a Cleaner Planet* (Cambridge, MA: The MIT Press, 2001).

Chapter 5   Endings and Beginnings
    1. BBC History — Henry Cavendish (1731–1810)
http://www.bbc.co.uk/history/historic_figures/cavendish_henry.shtml
    2. Charles Blagden, "Obituary of Henry Cavendish." *Gentlemen's Magazine*, March 1810, p. 292.

Glossary

bequest (bih-KWEST)—personal property or money designated for a specific purpose in a person's will.

carbon dioxide (CAR-bun dye-AWK-side)—a type of gas that extinguishes fire.

combustion (come-BUSS-chun)—the act of burning.

element (EH-leh-munt)—a substance that cannot be divided into other substances.

factitious air (fack-TIH-shus AIR)—gas that is caught in some other substance, that can be set free.

fixed air (FIKST AIR)—gas that will not burn, such as carbon dioxide.

hydrogen (HIGH-druh-jun)—an odorless, colorless, highly inflammable gas, the lightest of the elements and the most common.

inflammable (in-FLA-muh-bull)—something that is quick to burn.

meteorology (mee-tee-uh-RAH-luh-jee)—the study of weather.

mutton (MUH-tun)—the meat of a grown sheep.

phlogiston (floe-JISS-ton)—substance which was believed to be what made things burn.

torsion balance (TORE-shun BA-lunts)—suspended beam with equal weights at each end that is allowed to twist freely; used by Henry Cavendish to calculate the density of the Earth.

valet (va-LAY)—a male servant who does personal services for the man for whom he works.

For Further Reading

For Young Adults

Hayhurst, Chris. *Hydrogen Power of the Future: New Ways of Turning Fuel Cells into Energy*. New York: Rosen Publishing, 2003.

Uehling, Mark. *The Story of Hydrogen*. New York: Scholastic Library Publications, 1995.

Works Consulted

Aykroyd, W.R. *Three Philosophers (Lavoisier, Priestley and Cavendish)*. London: William Heinemann, 1935.

Blagden, Charles. "Obituary of Henry Cavendish," *Gentlemen's Magazine*, March, 1810, p. 292.

Henry, Lord Brougham. *Lives of Men of Letters and Science, Who Flourished in the Time of George III*. London: Charles Knight and Co., 1845.

Hoffmann, Peter. *Tomorrow's Energy: Hydrogen, Fuel Cells, and the Prospects for a Cleaner Planet*. Cambridge, MA: The MIT Press, 2001.

Jungnickel, Christa and Russell McCormmach. *Cavendish*. Philadelphia: The American Philosophical Society, 1996.

Knight, David M. *Science in the Romantic Era*. Aldershot, England: Ashgate Publishing, Ltd., 1998.

McCormmach, Russell. *Speculative Truth: Henry Cavendish, Natural Philosophy, and the Rise of Modern Theoretical Science*. London and New York: Oxford University Press, 2004.

Playfair, John. *The Works of John Playfair*. Edited by J.G. Playfair, 4 volumes, Edinburgh, Scotland: Publisher unknown, 1822.

Wilson, George. *The Life and Works of the Honorable Henry Cavendish*. London: The Cavendish Society, 1851.

On the Internet

Eric Weisstein's World of Scientific Biographies
http://scienceworld.wolfram.com/biography/Cavendish.html

BBC History - Henry Cavendish (1731–1810)
figures/cavendish_henry.shtml
www.bbc.co.uk/history/historic_figures/cavendish_henry.shtml

Biography of Henry Cavendish
http://mattson.creighton.edu/HistoryGasChemistry.html

Biography of Henry Cavendish/MIT University
http://chemistry.mtu.edu/~pcharles/SCIHISTORY/HenryCavendish.html

The Royal Society
http://www.royalsoc.ac.uk/

Hydrogen
http://pearl1.lanl.gov/periodic/elements/1.html

Index